GW00480784

Dedicated to Jane.
Thank you for passing on the keys to the kingdom.

Special thanks to Emma Sanderson and Bruce Hiscock for editorial support.

Prologue

As a marketer of over 14 years I have seen and experienced growth for all kinds of businesses, from using traditional marketing techniques through to the latest online hacks for paid advertising. I was pretty sure that my marketing skills were ALL I needed to grow my business and help others grow theirs.

I WAS SOOO WRONG!

And I am pretty pleased to have learnt that too. I thought that passing on my marketing skills to help people make more money, was my purpose and most valuable contribution to the world. It wasn't until I delved into the teachings of highly successful business and spiritual leaders that I discovered an entirely different perspective on business growth. I discovered that marketing formed only half of the equation for profitability and success - I also discovered that there was a large network of super successful business leaders that had already cottoned on to this.

They had discovered, that it was through investing in personal, spiritual and emotional growth that enabled the most powerful business growth.

By a series of 'coincidences' (though I now know there is no such thing) I was led off the beaten track, beyond the reality that I had allowed myself to believe was my 'market place', the place where I was meant to create my living and build my world, and I fell upon a network of highly successful entrepreneurs. These people seemed to possess the keys to the kingdom, creating a world full of knowledge, and in doing so, had created a life beyond their wildest dreams. I have experienced these sorts of people in different walks of life - not just business entrepreneurs, but all kinds of people that have discovered the secret to happiness through creating what they wanted in life - t5he secret to becoming a co-creator of their life. Through practicing simple techniques on a daily basis they were able to achieve the reality they sought.

Through this deep exploration, I opened up chunks of myself, that I had closed the door on for years believing that they served no purpose to my revenue generating, mortgage paying, home building, parental aspirations. Up until this point I had believed that you should 'stick to what you know' in order to make money and be successful. Let me tell you - this is the WORST advice you could give anyone, least of all yourself. The learning, the growing and the sheer magic of your potential exists way outside that comfort zone - WAY, WAY beyond what you believe to be your skillset and WAY beyond the world that you have been programming in your mind since the day you were born.

I'm glad to have discovered a wealth of literature, techniques and principles put together by the world's most successful people that have taken that curiosity and discovered the truth, the science and the facts around our existence. Stuff that frankly, I may spend the rest of my life learning and developing my knowledge on. However the amount I have picked up so far has enabled me to transform my life in a way that I never EVER thought someone "LIKE ME" would be able to, and in sharing what I have learnt I hope to be able to help others too.

August 2020 marks 12 years since I began my spiritual journey and in this book I unpack my journey thus far. Every THING, PERSON, EXPERIENCE AND ENCOUNTER that I now believe have led me to this turning point. The experiences I now realise 'happened for a reason' and have shaped EVERYTHING in my reality – though I wasn't aware of it at the time. I promise you that when you become aware of these forces working in your life and open your mind to these concepts, you won't be able to un-see them. You will start to notice these miracles daily, become a master of your reality and live a fulfilled and peaceful life. Through rediscovering my soul purpose and redefining my goals I have been able to experience life beyond my wildest dreams - and I'm told, the best is yet to come.

I hope this book will give you a taste of what's possible and enable you to believe in bigger and better experiences. Start living life to the full and learn how to co-create all your wishes, dreams and desires.
You deserve it!

Life is to be ENJOYED, not ENDURED!

Namaste.
Anoushka x

Square Peg, Round Hole

I remember watching films like 'The Truman Show' and having curiosity around the concept of parallel realities. Films like 'The Matrix' and a whole host of mind bending 'tales' that suggest there are other dimensions that we can quantum leap to in an instant. Ah – 'Quantum Leap'. I loved that show too! This stuff fascinated me as a youngster – but I kept a lid on my suspicions, because I didn't want you to think I was crazy! Funny how other people's opinion of me mattered so much back then.

Actually I have ALWAYS worried about what you thought of me. Crippled by the fear of not being heard or being misunderstood. It was easier to keep my thoughts and opinions locked inside. This fear became a blockage in me that I carried for years and toughened along the way. A blockage that I now understand to be one of the single greatest recipes for failure in life. Thankfully I was given the opportunity to peel back the layers of my soul, 'the onion' deep within me, and release these blockages. The first step was to look back a little...

I felt like the most awkward little 'square' brown girl growing up. Outwardly I was seen as a good girl in school, never got into trouble, made good grades, played the piano, studied dance and music and appeared very happy and creative. In reality I was full of shame inside, felt 'less than' and uncomfortable in my own skin. I struggled to communicate authentically. I felt lost and tried to shape myself to fit in with the people, places or situations I was in.
Looking back on that poor little girl I empathise with her. She was unable to see her true potential and as a result she was destined to fail.

Having studied Dance at university, I was surrounded by creative and passionate souls that had no shame about this chosen path - but somehow I always did. Perhaps it wasn't what society had presented as the most successful or wealthy profession, therefore it wasn't something to be proud of.

I have to say I feel horrified at myself for even thinking that. Such disproportionate ego and low self esteem. A 'superior worm', as my dear friend

Angela once described. I lived in a house with four other girls that I truly admired for having confidence in their chosen path and a general sense of joie de vivre. Why couldn't I behave this way? They seemed to be comfortable in their own skin and have a natural acceptance over themselves that I just didn't have. The perfectionist in me saw the faults in myself and never celebrated the qualities that made me, 'me'.

As a result I was never truly connected to source, to my purpose, to what I wanted out of life. I was misaligned. I was full of FEAR. I was constantly looking for ways to deny my truth and hide who I really was.

I became a progressively heavy drinker. Before I knew it, I was falling around drunk everywhere and humiliating myself and creating even more shame and guilt around my life. I remember being introduced to my brother's successful and happy friends some years later and trying to lie about the fact that I had studied Dance. I just wanted to be someone else. I was a square peg in a round hole.

By this point nothing I SAID was actually going to make people think I was a loser - all they had to do was look at the state of me to see that!

On leaving uni there was very little hope for me. I had bouts of cleaning up, trying my hand at an office temp job here and there but it wasn't long before my mis-aligned ego would destroy things again. I mean, didn't they know I was far too intelligent to be filing and making cups of tea? How very dare they fire me....! I stumbled through my early 20s like this. Hopeless, useless and wasted! The worse I got, the further away I got from my soul purpose, the further away I got from the source, the divine – my temple path. I had turned my back on religion long ago, despite my devout Catholic upbringing. I was ashamed of myself. There was never room for shame in the Catholic church I believed. I feared God and all things spiritual. I shut out any ideas that there could be a power greater than me. And thus the sunlight of the spirit was blocked and the door closed for good.

Waking up in a hospital bed for the umpteenth time, this time following a 48 hour coma may have awakened me a little – you would think? But with shame and guilt on overdrive now there was no way I could change. In fact, I had accepted that a slow alcoholic death was my destiny and THAT was one of the few things I didn't fear. Bring it on.

Better off dead. God, if you're out there - 'WHY AM I STILL HERE?', I thought. I couldn't wait to get out of the hospital to get another drink in me to get the job done.

My world was getting smaller. My eyes had died and so had my spirit. I was in the grips of a chronic spiritual malady. I was sick and tired of being sick and tired. After being to hell and back several times, on one uneventful day I was lead to experience something that would change my life forever.

"A wretch like me"

One Monday evening I threw on some clothes and wandered into a church hall, trembling from head to toe with an army of butterflies in my gut, rising up to my throat. I couldn't say much - I smoked like a chimney back then which helped keep my hands busy and allowed me to nod rather than speak to respond. I cant remember how I got there or why I was going. There had been countless attempts at recovery and rehabs before but somehow this was different. I saw beautiful, well dressed, clean, happy women that seemed to have life licked. I wanted that too. They had jobs, families, LIVES... surely they are nothing like me I thought. As the meeting went on I heard experience which I identified with, I heard strength which I wanted, and I got an amazing sense of hope.

One day at a time I began to absorb this stuff called 'recovery'. I went hours, days, weeks, months... then years without a drink and somehow I was doing ok. This was pretty miraculous for someone that couldn't go an hour without a drink. How was this happening?

I had a network of 'suggesters' - people who gave advice with no judgement. People who loved me unconditionally. People who I had a deep connection with on a level I had never experienced before. I had a community. They said find a sponsor, someone who you admire. She had golden hair and an aura of sunshine about her. She had a bounce in her walk and seemed fearless and relaxed. That's what I wanted, I thought to myself. From that moment on I did as I was told, because I wanted what she had. I trusted in the process through identifying with her and others around me. That was all the trust I needed then.

I learned how to connect with a higher power of my own making. I chose to call it GOD at first as that's what I knew. GOD took the form and shape of the Catholic God of my childhood as it was familiar and I didn't know any different. Some of my fellows referred to GOD as 'Group Of Drunks' didn't really matter how each of us perceived it. All that mattered was that I had opened my mind up to the realisation that there was a power greater than ME that could and would help if sought. That was the just the beginning.

The fellowship I had become a part of, shaped my existence for the next 11 years, allowing me to stay sober, which in turn allowed me to get great jobs and find success in my career. From the unemployable, arrogant youngster with an attitude problem to learning humility, grace and dignity - with the help of my beloved Jane. I moved up the corporate ladder quickly, learning and developing my skills. Rapidly chasing the next step up to make up for all that lost time I felt I had through the drinking years. This was my path now - this was my purpose. Life went from good to great. I had managed to create a 'normal looking life' despite the carnage of my dark past. I got married, pregnant, divorced and then bought my own home - in that order, all on my own, of my own self will, with my own skills, intelligence and hard work. WRONG! My self will was not creating all these wonderful things in my life - my self will was only good at getting me drunk. So how was it that my life had begun to transform? How did I suddenly develop the confidence and ability to become a wife, mother and successful marketer? What had shifted my direction and why?

There was a power greater than me working in my life despite not being aware of it. I simply did as I was told, practiced my programme daily, prayed, meditated (hmmm well, kinda) and attended meetings to connect with people and share what was going on for me. I began to connect to my inner truths and share openly and honestly. I was slowly unlocking my true self and accepting myself as I was.

The steps of recovery allowed me to heal the past, unblock my past limitations, forgive myself for my overwhelmingly low self esteem and believe in a better version of myself. I learned to reach out to a power greater than myself for guidance and do service, which I learned was about contributing to the lives of others. The most rewarding and purpose giving act of them all. It allowed me to discover my WHY? And I didn't even know it at the time!

The fellowship had embedded the foundations of living a life of purpose – a life of service to God. It was the beginning of my journey of spiritual and emotional growth that I had stunted the minute I took a drink of alcohol to change the way I felt. Now I was feeling my feelings, sharing my experiences, expressing my thoughts and emotions and accepting myself. This was the beginning of the journey to source.

Let go, Let God

One of the first things I learnt at the beginning of my spiritual journey was that I needed to TRUST. Trust in my higher power, Trust in the process, 'Let go, Let God', 'Ask and you shall receive' etc etc.

But no one told me HOW to trust. They said 'fake it till you make it' and in all honesty that worked in my early years of recovery as I didn't need to know WHY I was doing this stuff, I just knew it was working so I kept doing it. Some days the level of trust was higher than others but I kept 'chipping away' as advised by one of our old timers. But now, eleven years since my first rock bottom and the chips were down again. Unemployment, global pandemic, ill health, another failing relationship and fear, fear, fear...

I had gone right back to day one - a SOBER rock bottom.

I am a firm believer that when we reach bottom the ONLY way is up - I knew that YAZZ picture disc I bought back in the 80s would have some significance one day!

So I had a choice at this stage, to let go and give up, or 'let go and let God' with a firm intention and most importantly, TRUST. I remembered that old saying...

"God will move a mountain, but remember you have to bring the shovel"

With all the odds against me and an inevitable economic crisis ahead I decided to take action and build my own business and put my trust in God.

I should mention at this stage that embarking on anything of this kind is **way out of my comfort zone**. But somehow I trusted that it was going to be ok. I had heard along the way that the place outside your comfort zone is the place where the true magic happens. Where miracles, transformation and reinvention unfold. By stepping out fearlessly I let go of a dead weight of negative vibrations I was carrying. That bold step into the unknown propelled me into a state of high vibrational frequency - aka, hope, faith and trust!

Then followed a flurry of 'coincidences', from books, readings, people, places, things that had been handed to me during the lockdown. I would never have 'had the time' or the patience to take note whilst I was working full time and being a full time mum. Suddenly I was saying yes to things I normally wouldn't have time for. I was open to experiences, and I had been given the gift of time and space to grow. Opportunities for growth were effortlessly being drawn towards me. I was able to have gratitude for the opportunity to reshape my career and the re-address the balance in my life. It was that gratitude that propelled me further. Ideas and passions were beginning to flow from me with ease. Whilst the time and space had always existed for all the things I was now doing, I simply hadn't accessed it before. I began to realise that these 'coincidences' were a direct result of letting go of fear and living in the present moment. When I took the time to breathe and slow down and step forward with courage, inspiration came naturally. I was being shifted into alignment with source. All it takes is a moment in time to shift your vibrational frequency and jump into that parallel universe - and KEEP MOVING FORWARDS.

Daily rituals developed throughout this time, strengthening and reinforcing my spiritual beliefs and drawing me into further vibrational alignment with the divine. Through developing my knowledge of certain intricate spiritual concepts and techniques I was also able to remove some of the more deeply engrained negative limiting beliefs. This was the root cause of being 'stuck' in life. Common negative engrained beliefs such as 'I don't deserve, love, money, success' or 'money is the root of all evil' or 'successful people are just lucky' 'men always let me down' etc etc are what keep us where we are, and until we change the narrative, where we will remain. The solution to changing the narrative is clearing away the wreckage of past beliefs and accepting abundance in all areas of life. This involves consistent practice of a few techniques which I cover in more detail in the next chapter. I was now beginning to SEE, FEEL, HEAR and EXPERIENCE things I would have once overlooked. I was meeting people on a similar path and drawing new opportunities towards me. I started seeing signs and synchronicities such as feathers, butterflies, patterns and repeated numbers EVERYWHERE like the world just suddenly turned on in colour.

I now know these 'signs' are an indication that you are becoming aligned with the divine energies and therefore able to recognise guidance more clearly. I had 'coincidentally' felt drawn to dancing again, playing the piano, singing and cooking - the things I had always loved to do. Now I was feeling the freedom to experience them without ego or self-centred fear, without inhibition. These experiences were creating the high vibrational emotions that we so effortlessly access when we indulge in our divine gifts and unique talents – the things that make us feel most alive. Whilst I had locked this gifts away in a box, I was limiting my growth and potential for a life of abundance and joy.

Energy in Motion

I was now beginning to trust this concept of ENERGY and how like attracts like.

Emotion = energy in motion therefore any emotion, good or bad, will attract more of the same energy. So the emotions we generate have great power in manifesting our reality.

Consider this;

Ever started the day off on the wrong foot and then experienced one thing after another becoming increasingly irritating and unmanageable?

Woke up late! Rushing, anxious, panicked
Get in the car – no petrol. Get to petrol station and there's a queue – angry, impatient, more anxious.

Get on the M25 - TRAFFIC!!! ARGHHHHH! Angry, worried, going to get fired. Late for meeting. The boss will be angry with me...

Get to work and the entire day turns into an avalanche of stress, unmanageability and chaos.

Sound familiar?

Notice how one negative thought changed the dynamic of the entire day. Had he/she changed the narrative by letting go of the negative outcome that hadn't happened yet, things may have started like like this...

'I slept really well last night'
'Man, that was a good sleep, thank you God for my comfortable bed'.
'I pray for all those that don't have a nice warm bed.'

The frequencies of gratitude and love would be accessed and the day would have felt a whole lot different by attracting similar energies. This shift would have manifested an entirely different day.

Imagine how the day could have unfolded...

*Woke up late - **grateful** for waking up feeling refreshed.*
Go to get petrol and buy some sweet treats for colleagues
Extra few minutes causes traffic to move along.
Arrive at work five minutes late with treats for all.
Happy colleagues who all express their gratitude.
GRATITUDE ATTRACTS GRATITUDE.
Fantastic day at work.
Left a few minutes late to make up for the later start.
Smooth drive home with no traffic.
Home - happy and relaxed with loved ones.

I invite you to try a quick exercise to prove that ***everything*** in our reality can be moved through energy vibrations via emotions that we create.

Instant Manifestation exercise:
TRUSTING a power greater than yourself and one which we can't see or comprehend is easier said than done and I KNOW you, like myself, will want some instant PROOF of these energies in action. The challenge is for me was in the trusting at first (being naturally sceptical and self reliant), so it is important to fully and completely let go of the outcome. Don't obsess about it or even think about it again. The results are absolutely astonishing.

Here goes…

It's called the Two Cup method or 'Quantum Jumping'
Take two glasses. Fill one with water and leave one empty. Write your current situation on a post-it note and place it on the glass filled with water.
E.g. No money, or no relationship (choose one)
Label the other glass with a specific desired outcome
E.g. £3000, meet soul mate.

Hold the glass with the water in it and focus all your energy on the way that situation makes you feel. Transmit your vibrational frequencies of that disappointment, fear and low self worth into the glass. Hold that feeling for a while. AMPLIFY IT. Now, pour the water into the other glass slowly paying attention to the sound of the water and feel/visualise and imagine that money in your hand/bank account for example. Amplify that feeling as much as you possibly can. Then drink the water. Pop the post-it notes in the bin and put the glasses away and forget about it. DO NOT go looking around for whatever you asked for. TRUST. More will be revealed!

Journey to enlightenment

This is a topic of great depth but this chapter aims to break down the fundamental tools and tactics, in a way that is practical and applicable to daily life. It is important to understand that enlightenment doesn't happen over night - however, you can make changes today that will accelerate this journey. Remember that everything is made up of energy. The more you resist the concept of God/higher power/high vibrational energy/Divine source - then the harder it becomes to trust it and therefore manifest changes in your reality. Once you are able to wholeheartedly believe that, you are half way there.

Goal setting
If you want to change the narrative of your life and manifest a new reality RIGHT NOW you need to be clear about your goals. You must set intentions, pray or make your request to the universe in a clear and concise way but with enough flexibility to let the universe create on your behalf. Vision boards are a good way for you to depict certain goals to improve focus, but don't obsess over how

you will get there. Leave the finer details of the journey up to the universe. It is more important to select imagery that evokes emotion. That is the anchor that will enable you to crystallise that into existence. When your goals are set, commit them to writing and set a strategy, but again do not be too meticulous about the detail as this creates restriction. Now consider your 'WHY?'. When creating goals you must ensure that they benefit others as well as yourself. Self-centred aims come from EGO which is direct opposition to the laws of universal abundance. Now trust it's on its way and let it go. It is good practice to keep the strategy and/or vision board somewhere you can see it daily.

It is important to believe that the universe, God, creator, source or whatever you want to call it, has already created all that you desire - the dream home already exists or is in creation, the soul mate already exists, the sum of money, already exists - and it IS your divine right to have it. Contrary to some beliefs of God, it does not punish or reward, simply works in alignment with the frequencies you emit. You therefore need to align our vibrational frequencies with that of the goal state - the heightened state of existence. You need to be living and breathing in the space of high vibrational frequencies as much as you can in your day to naturally move into flow with the universe and therefore in flow with the intentions you have placed in its power.

The expression of love and pure joy emit the **highest** frequencies of all. Remember it's not just how we behave on the outside that counts. The state of our thoughts **is** intimately connected to our **emotional** condition and in turn, our physical reality. It works both ways so if we are harbouring resentments we are most certainly attracting that same energy towards us from others.

The following tools are practiced to ensure that we are continuously improving our spiritual condition and raising our vibrations on a daily basis.

Affirmations
At first, the concept of meditation and complete stillness of the mind was too difficult for me. I had had an incredibly busy and unproductive mind for so long. A butterfly brain, fluttering around restlessly, always focussed on multiple goals and dreams and wasting immense amounts of energy

on negative self talk. These 'habits' needed to be 'undone' and reprogrammed before a meditative state could be achieved.

I was introduced to meditation in a local group I attended on a Friday where we would read prayers from our beloved scripture then sit quietly for 12 minutes. I used this time to run through affirmations in my mind. Affirmations are positive statements declaring specific goals in their completed states in the present moment in time. The concept of recreating your reality is about reprogramming your belief system to believe that the goal has been reached and being grateful for the present moment. I would say these affirmations to myself during my 12 minute meditation to calm my mind and feed positive suggestions to my mind. Much like a mantra – they seemed to evoke a sense of peace. This was not meditation, but this technique was just what I needed at the time where some deep reprogramming needed to be done before I could find peace. This is a very tricky concept to master at first, because the logical brain wants to intervene and tell you it isn't true - so begin with gratitude for the things that already exist. Thank you for my beautiful home, car, hair, skin etc. Be grateful for the very thing that you desire an abundant or elevated version of.

Once you are able to establish gratitude and experience how that shifts the perspective of your current reality you can then grow that belief and form new realities.

They say that 21 days is the amount of time it takes to form a habit. I believe it took a bit longer for me as I needed to break old habits of thought first - ones that were very stubborn and deeply engrained!

It is at the most rested state that the subconscious mind is most receptive to imprinting and reprogramming beliefs and so has the power to create new realities. Stating that which you desire repeatedly whilst in this state has a profound effect on the mind. To coin a well known phrase *'I think, therefore I am'*, Descartes. We are the manifestations of what we create through thoughts and emotions connected to thoughts.

Here are some examples of powerful affirmations that you can choose from. Choose what resonates with you, reword or be more specific where possible but keep them short so that you can memorise them easily. Affirmations are best used in the early morning and before bed when your mind is at its most receptive state. You may want to set your affirmations to come on as your alarm clock. This is a very powerful way to ease into the day.

- *I love and approve of myself as I am*
- *I accept myself as I am*
- *I release any self doubt or limiting belief*
- *I release any resentments towards.....and I wish them love and peace*
- *I let go of resentment, worry and anxiety that no longer serves me*
- *I am at peace with myself*
- *I draw opportunities towards me*
- *Money comes easily and naturally to me now*
- *I have more than enough money to meet all my needs and desires*
- *There are opportunities coming to me in expected and unexpected ways*
- *I am in divine connection with my soul mate now*
- *I release any fear around receiving or giving love*
- *I release any fear of success or money*
- *I am successful*
- *I am powerful*
- *I am beautiful*
- *I radiate positivity to all those that I meet*
- *I forgive myself for my past*

I invite you to affirm your goals and create your own affirmations. The act of writing further affirms the beliefs and commits them to your subconscious in a powerful way.

GOALS	WHY?

Affirmations

Practice the affirmations consistently until they become your new narrative. No matter what you have done or how much carnage you have created in life, everyone deserves a second chance but it begins when you believe that you deserve it. Affirmations were a tool for 'faking it to make it' in my early recovery. I didn't believe these words to begin with as I was much more familiar with the negative, destructive self talk. Slowly but surely I began to say my affirmations with a smile on my face, with absolute belief that this was true. It is only when I look back that I appreciate how they have transformed so many seemingly hopeless states. It is invaluable to look back - but don't stare. Look back only to remind yourself how far you've come and super power your gratitude to the next level!

Prayer
Praying means different things to different people, religions and beliefs. I'm going to break down prayer into its simplest form. Prayer to me, is conversation with my higher power - the power that creates the path ahead. In order to be in the flow of all good things provided by the divine we need to remain connected. Like a relationship with a good friend. If a friendship is to get stronger we

need to put in the action and see to it that the relationship is nurtured through conversation and regular contact. Lack of communication means lack of direction and the opportunity for that message to land will simply shift to someone else that is open to receive it.

Much like affirmations the wording is key. If your prayers are worded in a way that describes a sense of lack (lack of money, love, success) then unfortunately that will remain the case. The universe picks up on the most prevalent energy so use the most positive words to pray with. If you are focussed on debt you will attract more debt. So instead thank the universe for the things of value that you have. Gratitude is the ULTIMATE HACK to instant happiness. Pray for all that you are grateful for, write your prayers down and see it, feel it and AMPLIFY it - and practice it daily and in doing so you attract more of it.

Contribution, service and giving creates another magical vibrational frequency. Therefore praying for others amplifies the divine connection and gets you back in the flow state with the divine. You have to give it away to keep it. In praying for someone to have more love, peace or money in their life, you match the frequency of receiving the same things for yourself.

Giving is easy when we love someone but how about those that have hurt us?
When you have a deep resentment over the person that abandoned you, the person that fired you, the person that stole your peace of mind the ULTIMATE solution is to...
pray for them!
Pray that all peace, love and abundance will come to them. This act of giving shifts the negative frequency, instantly protecting you from more of the same and miraculously the resentment disappears - like MAGIC! Try praying for someone right now. Notice how you feel. Repeat it daily. Notice the shift.

I should mention that the concept of praying for someone that hurt me was a concept I was very reluctant to try. I did as I was told and prayed for my ex-husband - through gritted teeth at first. Daily and nightly. Could barely face him at one point. Until one day the resentment had lifted. The external situation had shifted to match the love and peace I was wishing him. In return I had peace in my heart and no longer a single bad feeling towards him. We co-parent our son in absolute harmony with love and trust and we respect one another's lives. It has rippled across our families and dissolved a lot of the pain and upset that had been caused by our split. This has had a directly positive impact on our son who has never had to experience any negative energies between his parents - well not that he can remember!

Meditation
There is an array of powerful books and scriptures that describe the art of meditation beautifully. Some of which will resonate and others that wont.

There are also lots of guided meditations that you can listen to on YouTube or on free apps available now. Rather than quote from every book I have read on the topic or recommend apps from an abundant market of such tools I will describe meditation in the way that has helped me. I am not a yogi, but who knows, maybe one day I will be. I have simply practiced the discipline of meditation and experimented with a variety of techniques and selected those that work for me. I like to keep it simple.

First step is breath.
Get into a comfortable position. To begin with lying down is perfectly acceptable. Naturally you will begin to feel more connected to source in an upright position aligning the chakras towards the earth's core.
Notice the way you are lying or sitting down. Take a deep breath in through your nose, expanding your abdominal area and out again through your nose, pulling your abdominal muscles in towards your back. Practice this 10 times. After each breath go deeper into relaxation.

Next - noticing your physical self.

Once your breathing has taken you deep into relaxation, notice your body, the weight of the body on the bed or chair, the temperature, the sensations. Focus your energies towards one of your index fingers. Notice the pulsing or tingling sensations. Continue to breathe, slowly and deliberately.

Practice taking your focus from one finger to the other and amplifying the energy and focus. Once you are able to do this easily and effortlessly try focussing on each of the 7 chakras of the body and visualise the colours connected to them.

Root – base of the spine –red
Sacral – lower abdominal area - orange
Solar Plexus – the central core - gold
Heart – in the centre of the chest - green
Throat – neck – blue
Third Eye –centre of the forehead - indigo
Crown – top of the head - purple

Whilst practicing the scanning of chakras and focusing on colour energies you are taking your focus away from 'what am I going to make for dinner' or 'what time do I need to pick the kids up', or 'did I add washing powder to the Ocado order'. This deviation is the first step in stopping the noise and finding calm, and from there your meditation muscles can fine tune.

Another form of focus is to bring in a simple mantra such as SO HUM. There are a number of Sanskrit mantras that align blissfully with the breath rhythm. Deepak Chopra's 21 day abundance mediation is a beautiful and simplistic programme that gently guides you in to complete stillness, allowing you to 'go within' easily and effortlessly. As the days go by you will find that the time just slips away and you emerge feeling energised. It is a discipline I intend to improve on daily as I trust that it harmonises my energies creating a channel for the divine to direct me to the flow state. That place where life is easy and effortless!

Visualisation

A truly remarkable tool if used correctly, is the art of visualisation of a specific goal. Visualisations access creative nodes in the brain that naturally tap into the emotional self when you add detail to the imagery and bring the scenario to life. In order to get to the right place for visualisations to take shape it is useful to have practiced some form of meditation first. Guided mediations form a good basis for practicing this technique and enable you to imagine more vividly and creatively.

Visualisation starts from being able to picture your dream house, dream car or dream partner but in order to imprint that into your psyche it needs emotional energy and the optimum state of mind. The optimum state of mind is at a very relaxed state – usually just before bed when your subconscious is most receptive to suggestions e.g. after a long bath and a mediation with some soothing music, candles and aromatherapy. Then be clear about the outcome you want to manifest. The details are important. Use this opportunity to get creative. What are the colours, smells, textures.

Who is in the picture? Can you see what they are wearing, saying, doing. Bring the image to life. Now pump up the emotion. Energy in motion. How do you feel up on that stage singing to thousands of people? How does it FEEL winning that race or match? AMPLIFY THAT FEELING. Now at the point where you are in the most heightened phase of the visualisation ANCHOR THE FEELING. Press your thumb and your forefinger together and hold it for 17 seconds. And release. Come back into the room and slowly drift off to sleep.

There are a number of techniques that I have merged into that sequence. Some of you may recognise the NLP and hypnotherapy concepts there. Many successful sportsmen and women, actors, entrepreneurs and political leaders have used these sorts of techniques to prepare for high pressured situations and as a result of their success continue to do so in all areas of their lives to create more abundance, creativity, love and joy.

It's not working - I give up!

These techniques when practiced consistently and correctly WILL create the life you desire. BUT there are some common mistakes. For example, visualisations can be a good way to set the ultimate goal but how do we know if we are heading down the right path if we are not seeing results instantly. Let's look at the two cup method again. Some of you, since practicing this exercise may have already met your soul mate or manifested a sum of money. Fantastic! Feels amazing doesn't it? Others may not have- or may not think they have - but were you open to receiving it when it arrived? Here are the common mistakes.

Mistake #1 – the watched pot. If we are constantly waiting and thinking about the outcome, we are not living in the present and we are not living in trust. The sense of urgency we create while we are desperately waiting for the phone to ring to say we got the job, or checking to see if a person has messaged, or checking our bank account every five minutes, we are sending off negative energies and pushing the outcome further away. Not trusting means not living in the now. The NOW is where the signs are found.
The thing that you thought you wanted to receive may have been packaged in a slightly different form. So, your soul mate didn't fall on your doorstep, but perhaps that errand you didn't run for a friend earlier in the week may have been the opportunity to bump into your soul mate. You missed your delivery and now it's being delivered elsewhere!

Mistake #2: Not having a clear intention. If you are constantly just wishing for your business to be a success but haven't thought about what that looks like, you are inviting too many varieties of that request. Be specific about the goal but flexible about the journey towards it. Reverse engineer the entire journey from the amount of money you want the business to generate to the number of opportunities you need to achieve and date stamp it. Otherwise you could be on the right path – but a long one! Now to speed that up – practice all the tools and techniques. Stay mindful, stay present, stay open to receive. Give freely and openly the things that you would like to receive and give with love. The minute you fall out of line with your authentic self you fall out of flow.

Mistake #3: Balance. Fill your day with ALL the things you need to help your spirit grow. Create variety and allow space for maximum opportunity for miracles in your day. Don't stay glued to your work, or tv or other single focussed activity. Pause. Breathe and fill up on the energies around you. Laugh more, sing more, talk more. Be present with those that you love and don't take a single thing for granted. These moments are where the magic is hidden. Staying in the now and giving time, patience and love to those around you generates the best return of them all. Peace of mind. That place again – where life is easy and manageable and there is no stress. Stress is the number one killer in our society. It the the most damaging energy on our vital organs which is the cause of heart and brain trauma or illness.

Mistake #4: Lack of persistence.
If you give up at the first hurdle you catapult yourself back into the abyss of failure, self pity and stagnation. Certain 'failures' could also be perceived as the universe positioning you onto a better trajectory for your goals. Perhaps the person, place thing or situation you had hoped to manifest was not in alignment with the greater good. Trust it wasn't right for you and keep trudging on. That courage, that persistence and that resilience will super power you to shift your aim with great gusto which will draw that target to your arrow. Release the failure mentality, which chooses to blame the person, place, thing or situation that 'let you down'. Release the fear of humiliation, fear of criticism, and fear of making the same mistake again - if you're fearing it, you're manifesting it. Use the tools to unblock these negativities and reassess the situation that went wrong. Then, leverage the experience and be grateful for the new knowledge you have gained and power through. ALL of the great thinkers, leaders and entrepreneurs had to face this and

they all found success through leveraging that defeat to create the next step towards their growth.

Mistake #5: Self doubt.
The most destructive of them all - but the most difficult to change. I have a strong tendency to negative self belief. Many of my fellows refer to it as being 'wired up wrong'. True to a certain extent - but changeable for sure. This is why the tools need practicing on a daily basis. Self doubt has the ability to slow down your path to success and in extreme cases - sabotage your efforts entirely. We often do not even realise it's happening, as this self doubt sits in that dark node in the brain called the cerebellum which has such power over the rest of our behaviours. For some, the tools outlined in this book are not enough to re-route these habitual patterns of thought. More intrusive techniques can be used, such as hypnosis, CBT (cognitive behavioural therapy) and NLP (neuro-linguistic programming). There are a number of highly skilled practitioners and coaches that will work with you to tackle these issues at the core using one or a number of these techniques in a bespoke programme for your needs. I would always highly recommend investing in the creation of the best

version of yourself. When you invest in yourself you are telling the universe you deserve the best. The return will be better growth and success for yourself and those you serve - so definitely money well spent!

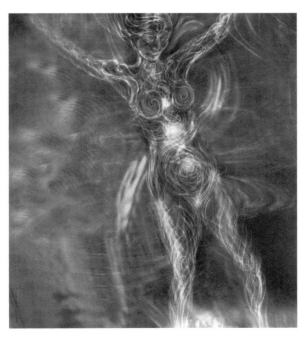

Dance like nobody is watching...

The dark side of enlightenment

It would be wrong of me not to mention that the journey to a more heightened spiritual awareness has its challenges. Before the world switched on in colour for me it went to a dark place. Whilst I had dealt with the past during the 4th and 5th steps of my early recovery there were repeated patterns of guilt, shame, resentment and low self esteem that needed to be worked on continuously. The 12 step programme of my recovery enabled me to keep working on my defects of character one day at a time in order to keep me sober - and that it did. However, during the second phase of spiritual awakening I had begun to experience some 11 years later I became affected by some deeply painful reflections of myself. I describe this as a 'sober rock bottom' earlier on. These emotions were pouring out in ways I had not experienced before. Anger, rage, deep regret, guilt, sadness and self loathing. I was having restless nights, waking up in cold sweats at funny times of the night, 1:11, 3:33, 1:23, 2:22 and suffering palpitations and what felt like raging heartburn and dizzy spells in the night. I was becoming physically moved by my external reality it seemed. It felt like I was shifting between my internal and external states and feeling very unsettled. I am now completely accepting of angel or spiritual encounters in the night. I am now more trusting of the process and therefore not afraid. My intuition went from curious to a sense of knowing and from fear to a deep trust and I was accepting the signs and symbols - the miracles, as completely normal, which they are.

The more you listen, you more you hear. The more connected you become with your self and your higher power, the more intense this dark phase will feel but just know that you are on the right path and it is a safe one. It gave me the opportunity to release a deeper level of fear and self acceptance of my shadow self.

It is a reassuring sign that you are heading to a really peaceful place so just keep pedalling! Use the time to explore your creativity and express yourself in ways that make you feel empowered and connected to source. For me, this was a period where I reconnected with Dance and Music improvisation and began exploring Chakra Dance, crystal therapies and Reiki and read more and more. I would encourage you to express yourself on paper too. I had many angel experiences and times where my imagination was more vivid and colourful and it was necessary for me to embrace all of these experiences as I believe they were divinely timed within my journey.

Here is one such piece of writing that was incredibly healing to write. It describes the realisation of my shadow self and the process as it revealed itself to me.

The Temple Path

The spirit calls again
She walks in her sleep
Meandering through the woods
Where it was buried as a child
Her joy, trust and hope
The tears fell suddenly, unexpectedly, without
warning
Cold, dark and damp
The leaves crunch.

A dragonfly swoops
She stops, turns her gaze
Down into the undergrowth
The shifting carpet of the forest
Deep beyond the temple path
Where it lands
Upon a giant onion
Cowering apologetically beside the path
She pulls at the layers
Crying harder now, with rage
Revealing rotten, damaged and pungent layers
Disintegrating between her fingers
Tearing, ashamedly, desperately
Screaming uncontrollably

Whilst reaching deep into its core
Engulfed.

A golden white light burns to touch
Blindingly hypnotic
Locked into a warm gaze
Overwhelming
Intense
She recognises the warmth
It's safe
It's home
The light engulfs her,
Comforts her
Radiating beauty, love, passion, eternity.

The mulch has disappeared
The path lights up
Step by step up the enchanted pathway
Surrounded by golden white light
She knows now
Reaching out to tap his chest to leave her mark
before he forgets.

She journeys back
Down the temple path
Slowly
Serenely

Trusting
Safely home
Awakened, free from the bondage of self and fear
Alive with the hope of a new beginning.

I didn't realise this was what I wanted to express until I wrote it. I have purposely kept it unabridged and straight from the heart as I feel that is where the power was captured. I simply had the urge to write and so I did. When this happens it is as though there is a direct calling from spirit wanting to communicate through me. There may not be any literary genius about this piece of writing, but it served the purpose of self expression and unblocked some hidden energies within me. Creativity is one of the most powerful channels to connecting to your higher self. Whether your creative passions are in fixing broken objects, singing in the shower or cooking - use this creativity to tap into your soul and celebrate just being you.

Life beyond your wildest dreams

These concepts, if practiced consistently will become second nature. The two cup method never fails to astonish me and the more you practice the better you will become at it. It's a good tool to keep reminding you why you are doing all of this work. Helps you stay focussed on the longer term goals even if there have been no obvious indications that it was on its way for quite a while. The things that 'fail' along the way can make or break your progress. So, you didn't get that job or that lottery win. To get angry, upset or frustrated is to misalign and push you further off track. It is so important to recognise that it is possible that this specific wish was not the optimum next step to your desired end goal. Remember the universe wants what is best for you and you must trust that. That specific manifestation may have appeared or variations of that which you requested, but you overlooked it as you were not focussing on "the now". It is important to practice acceptance as a solution. Acceptance is the most gratifying solution to every situation that hasn't gone as you would have liked it to go. Accept that God/the universe has your back and then you will find peace in the present situation as being exactly as it is meant to be at the present moment in time. Trust that all that you intend is already in existence and ready for you to receive. Just concentrate on always being receptive.

As human begins we are likely to feel disappointment, sadness, grief and pain and we cannot deny these feelings as they are a part of life. What we can do is accept them, feel the feelings, let them go and move on. To deny is like forcing them back into a bottle and shoving the cork down and letting the feelings ferment. Eventually those gasses will expand, those emotions will mature and the cork will fly. That is the very reaction that throws us right away from our temple path, our path to spirit.

Finding our soul purpose is discovering our true selves and our unique gifts. It is choosing that message, that talent or skill that will be of most service to humankind. According to world renowned speaker and coach, Tony Robbins, this is described as one of the six core human needs –

contribution. We need to contribute in order to have purpose and gain the ultimate spiritual fulfilment.

The most God centred way of contributing is to use our God-given, unique gifts. Perhaps your own experience, struggles you have overcome or pain you have dealt with is your greatest power and can be of service in helping others. Perhaps your talents can bring joy to those that need up-lifting. Perhaps you provide a service that lifts people out of poverty. The need to give, care, protect and serve others aligns with the divine and ultimate high vibrational energies and in return gives peace, serenity and joy. This is the ultimate life satisfaction from which all abundance flows freely and effortlessly.

We truly can have everything we desire in life provided we know ourselves, understand our purpose and put into action our contribution with love and gratitude. Life is one big, continuous circle of giving and receiving energy. Be thankful for who and what is in your life, and abundance and prosperity will flow freely back towards you.

About the Author

Anoushka Farouk was born in Surrey, UK in 1979. Daughter of two hard working parents Denise and Michael Farouk, sister to Adrian Farouk and mother to Jayden Mootoosamy. Anoushka is a Business Growth Entrepreneur and certified Spiritual Prosperity Coach leading entrepreneurs to connect with their purpose and achieve success. Anoushka plays the piano, practices Dance Movement Therapy, Chakra Dance and Oracle card reading.

Bibliography

The Alchemist. Paul Coelho.1988

The Monk Who Sold His Ferrari. Robin Sharma.1997

7 Spiritual Laws of Success. Deepak Chopra 1996

The Key to Living the Law of Attraction. Jack Canfield. 2014

The Power of the Subconscious Mind. Joseph Murphy. 1963

The Twelve Steps and Twelve Traditions. Alcoholics Anonymous. 1952

The Secret. Rhonda Burn 2006

The Language of Letting Go. Melody Beatie. 1990

Drop the Rock. Sara S., Todd W. 2005

A Year of Miracles. Marianne Williamson. 2011

The Prophet. Kahlil Gibran. 1923

The Big Book. Bill. W. 1939

Think and Grow Rich, Napoleon Hill.1937

Set it and Forget it. Eric Ho.2019

Transform your Life. K. Gyatso.2001

The Power of NOW. Eckhart Tolle.2001

Create Wealth and Abundance. Glenn Harold.2016

The Power of positive thinking. Norman Vincent Peale.1953

Twenty Four Hours a Day. Richmond Walker.2011

Creative Visualisation. Shakti Gawain.1978

Influencers:
Deepak Chopra
Bill Wilson
Master Sri Akarshana

Joe Vitali
Bob Proctor
Jake Ducey
Vishen Lakhiani
Robin Sharma
Marisa Peer
Abraham Hicks
Tony Robbins
Lee Harris
Paul Coelho
Jack Canfield
Jane
My warrior sisters
The fellowship of Alcoholics Anonymous
My mum

Printed in Great Britain
by Amazon

54902031R00037